"This generation of Christians inhabit cultures that sometimes reject not only biblical revelation about reality, but also the reality of reality itself. The Questions for Restless Minds series poses many of the toughest questions faced by young Christians to some of the world's foremost Christian thinkers and leaders. Along the way, this series seeks to help the Christian next generation to learn how to think biblically when they face questions in years to come that perhaps no one yet sees coming."

—Russell Moore,

public theologian, *Christianity Today*

"If you're hungry to go deeper in your faith, wrestle with hard questions, and are dissatisfied with the shallow content on your social media newsfeed, you'll really appreciate this series of thoughtful deep dives on critically important topics like faith, the Bible, friendship, sexuality, philosophy, and more. As you engage with some world-class Christian scholars, you'll be encouraged, equipped, challenged, and above all invited to love God more with your heart, soul, mind, and strength."

—Andy Kim,

multiethnic resource director, InterVarsity Christian Fellowship

What Is the Bible?

Questions for Restless Minds

Questions for Restless Minds

How Should Christians Think about Sex? ✦ Christopher Ash

What Does Nature Teach Us about God? ✦ Kirsten Birkett

Who Is Jesus of Nazareth? ✦ Craig L. Blomberg

How Do We Talk with Skeptics? ✦ Sam Chan

What Is the Bible? ✦ Graham A. Cole

What Is a Christian Worldview? ✦ Graham A. Cole

How Do We Know God Exists? ✦ William Lane Craig

What Does It Mean to Be a Thoughtful Christian? ✦ David S. Dockery

Why Does Friendship Matter? ✦ Chris L. Firestone and Alex H. Pierce

Who Chose the Books of the New Testament? ✦ Charles E. Hill

How Do We Live in a Digital World? ✦ C. Ben Mitchell

What Is Islam? ✦ Chawkat Moucarry

Are All Religions True? ✦ Harold A. Netland

How Do Humans Flourish? ✦ Danielle Sallade

How Should We Think about Gender and Identity? ✦ Robert S. Smith

How Can We Help Victims of Trauma and Abuse? ✦
Susan L. and Stephen N. Williams

How Should We Think about Homosexuality? ✦ Mark A. Yarhouse

What Is the Bible?

Graham A. Cole

D. A. Carson,
Series Editor

What Is the Bible?
Questions for Restless Minds, edited by D. A. Carson

Lexham Press, 1313 Commercial St., Bellingham, WA 98225
LexhamPress.com

Print ISBN 9781683595137
Digital ISBN 9781683595144
Library of Congress Control Number 2021937693

Lexham Editorial: Todd Hains, Abigail Stocker, Mandi Newell
Cover Design: Brittany Schrock
Interior Design and Typesetting: Abigail Stocker

The Christ on Campus Initiative exists to inspire students on college and university campuses to think wisely, act with conviction, and become more Christlike by providing relevant and excellent evangelical resources on contemporary issues.

Visit christoncampuscci.org.

Contents

Series Preface

D. A. CARSON, SERIES EDITOR

THE ORIGIN OF this series of books lies with a group of faculty from Trinity Evangelical Divinity School (TEDS), under the leadership of Scott Manetsch. We wanted to address topics faced by today's undergraduates, especially those from Christian homes and churches.

If you are one such student, you already know what we have in mind. You know that most churches, however encouraging they may be, are not equipped to prepare you for what you will face when you enroll at university.

It's not as if you've never known any winsome atheists before going to college; it's not as if you've never thought about Islam, or the credibility of the New Testament documents, or the nature of friendship, or gender identity, or how the claims of Jesus sound too exclusive and rather narrow, or the nature of evil. But up until now you've probably thought about such things within the shielding cocoon of a community of faith.

Now you are at college, and the communities in which you are embedded often find Christian perspectives to be at best oddly quaint and old-fashioned, if not repulsive. To use the current jargon, it's easy to become socialized into a new community, a new world.

How shall you respond? You could, of course, withdraw a little: just buckle down and study computer science or Roman history (or whatever your subject is) and refuse to engage with others. Or you could throw over your Christian heritage as something that belongs to your immature years and buy into the cultural package that surrounds you. Or—and this is what we hope you will do—you could become better informed.

But how shall you go about this? On any disputed topic, you do not have the time, and probably not the interest, to bury yourself in a couple of dozen volumes written by experts for experts. And if you did, that would be on *one* topic—and there are scores of topics that will grab the attention of the inquisitive student. On the other hand, brief pamphlets with predictable answers couched in safe slogans will prove to be neither attractive nor convincing.

So we have adopted a middle course. We have written short books pitched at undergraduates who want arguments that are accessible and stimulating, but invariably courteous. The material is comprehensive enough that it has become an important resource for pastors and other campus leaders who devote their energies to work with students. Each book ends with a brief annotated bibliography and study questions, intended for readers who want to probe a little further.

Lexham Press is making this series available as attractive print books and in digital formats (ebook and Logos resource). We hope and pray you will find them helpful and convincing.

1

INTRODUCTION

WEDDINGS CAN BE such fun, can't they? And they come in all shapes and sizes from huge to intimate, from casual to formal. The last wedding I attended was a classic Southern one where the bride had eleven bridesmaids. The setting was on a mountain and the feast afterwards was by a mountain lake. My wife especially appreciated the occasion. She is a fashion designer and for a time ran her own bridal business. One dress she sold was to a couple with an Armenian heritage, and we were invited to the wedding in their Armenian Orthodox Church. What a spectacle! Robes, incense, color and pageantry. What struck me in particular was how the priest held the Bible. It was handled with silk cloth. Human hands were not to touch the sacred book. What made this book so precious to him? Personal conviction? Tradition? That experience of the Armenian wedding raises for me the question of why value this ancient book.

Let's begin our exploration of this last question by considering the stories of two very different people who found transformative value in the pages of this famous book, a book that understood them—at least that is the claim.[1]

2

TWO STORIES: ONE FRENCH, ONE AMERICAN

ÉMILE CAILLIET WAS raised in a naturalistic environment in France. In fact, he first saw a Bible at the age of twenty-three. He had a longing though for self-understanding. He expresses that longing in powerful terms when he writes: "During long night watches in the foxholes [in WWI] I had in a strange way been longing—I must say it, however queer it may sound—for a book that would understand me. But I knew of no such book."[2] So what did Cailliet do? He set out to construct one himself: "Now I would in secret prepare one for my own private use."[3] Over time he constructed his book made up of quotations drawn from literature and philosophy. In the end, however, when he read his compilation he found only disappointment: "It carried no strength of persuasion."[4] Instead of insight he found emptiness.

Around that same time his wife happened on a Protestant church, went in and met the elderly pastor. As Cailliet relates the story: "She walked to his desk and *heard herself* say. Have you a Bible in French?"[5] Indeed he did. And Cailliet's wife upon his return home gave him the copy of the Bible. (How she found this church is an interesting story in itself.) He vividly describes what happened next:

> I literally grabbed the book and rushed to my study with it. I opened it and chanced upon the Beatitudes [Matthew 6]: I read, and read. ... I could not find words to express my awe and wonder. And suddenly the realization dawned upon me: This *was* the Book that would understand me! I needed it so much, yet, unaware I had attempted to write my own—in vain. ... I continued to read deeply into the night, mostly from the gospels. ... A decisive insight flashed through my whole being the following morning as I probed the opening chapters of the gospel according to John. The very clue to the secret of human life was disclosed right there, not stated in the foreboding language of philosophy, but in the common everyday language of human circumstances.[6]

Cailliet went on to become a noted philosopher and Christian thinker.

John Piper's story is different from that of Cailliet. Piper was raised by parents who prized the Bible and sought to live by it. He became a theological educator and eventually an influential author, speaker, and pastor. Over the years his belief in the Bible's truthfulness was challenged, particularly in graduate school. However, he discovered through experience that it was not so much him holding on to the Bible as an authority in his life but rather he was being held by it.

What held him? How can you be held by a book? Piper explores a number of metaphors in answering the question:

> The Bible was never like a masterpiece hanging in a museum that I viewed this way and that. Rather, it was like a window. Or like binoculars. My view *of* the Bible was always *through* the Bible. So when I say that, all along the way, my view was getting clearer and brighter and deeper, I mean the reality seen through it was getting clearer and brighter and deeper. *Clearer* as the edges of things became less fuzzy, and I could see how things fit together rather than just smudging into each other. *Brighter* as the beauty and impact of the whole message [of the Bible] was more and more attractive. And *deeper* in the sense of depth perspective—I suppose photographers would say "depth of Field." Things stretched off into eternity with breathtaking implications—in both directions past and future. You could sum it up with the phrase *the glory of God*. That's what I was seeing.[7]

For Piper, it was the Bible's vista of reality holding him and not the other way around.

Cailliet and Piper began in very different places. One started as a naturalist and the other was raised in a Christian home environment. Both came to the same place of prizing the book that understood them.

3

SUCH INSIGHT IN A BOOK

MY ARGUMENT IS that in the Bible insight can be found which can transform a human life. It did mine. So what are the insights I am talking about? What is the understanding that captured Cailliet's imagination and what is the vista of which John Piper speaks? Let me put it this way: this book helps me to see afresh, and with insight comes understanding. Moreover, this book addresses a number of our needs posed by the simple fact of a human existence in all its finiteness.

First, we see God afresh.

I heard this story about a preacher in Hyde Park, London. There is a famous section of the Park known as Speakers' Corner. Anyone can get up on a box and speak on any subject as long as no law is broken in doing so. One Sunday, there was a preacher who was confronted by an angry atheist who shouted out that he did not believe in God. The preacher replied, "Tell me about this God you don't believe in. I might not believe in him either." In our pluralist setting we can't assume that when the word "God" is spoken that we are all on the same page. To do so is a big mistake these days. So what God am I writing about?

The God I am writing about is the one that the Bible presents in its pages.[8] I wear glasses for driving and without them all is blurry. My glasses make all the difference. Color is sharper, shapes are well defined. I am not a menace on the road. John Calvin, a famous Christian leader of the past, employed the useful metaphor of the Bible described as a pair of glasses. He wrote:

> Just as old and bleary-eyed men and those with weak vision, if you thrust before them a most beautiful volume, even if they recognize it to be some sort of writing, yet can scarcely construe two words, but with the aid of spectacles will begin to read distinctly; so Scripture, gathering up the otherwise confused knowledge of God in our minds, having dispersed our dullness, clearly shows us the true God.[9]

For Calvin, the Bible was not an end in itself but a means to an end. This book showed him God.

The Bible brings God into focus. It did so for me. Before I started reading it I had the vaguest notion of God. God was the idea that there was a something behind everything. So what did I find? In its pages I found stories of God the creator who made creatures (Gen 1), God the judge who holds human beings accountable for their actions (Gen 11), God the rescuer who saves people (Exod), and God the restorer who will one day make the world right (Rev 21–22). These stories, I saw, centered on Jesus Christ (the four Gospels) and in so doing one big story emerges. I have more to say on that a little while later in this book.

In terms of God's character, I discovered two terms that summed up that character: "light" and "love." Both ideas are found in one of the brief letters found in the New Testament. In 1 John 1 we read the claim that God is light and in him there is no darkness at all. What is John talking about? In context, John is claiming that God is morally pure all the way through. "Holy" is the classic term. Personally speaking, I find this extremely important. I don't think that I want to trust a God who is only power. I might find myself submitting to sheer power. Prisoners of war had to do that to survive. So what can nuance power? That's where love comes into play. John also claims that God is love (1 John 4). He grounds this claim on the story of Jesus. The coming of Jesus into the world and his dying that we might live show us what God's love looks like. It is sacrificial. It removes the barrier between God and ourselves if we are willing to embrace it. I can trust a good God who loves me and who has done something about the brokenness of the world and promises that there is day coming when right will prevail (2 Pet 3).

Second, we see ourselves afresh.

Knowing who you are is not a new quest. The saying "Know yourself" was inscribed on the walls of the Temple of Apollo at Delphi in ancient Greece. Last century, existentialist writer and philosopher Jean Paul Sartre was bleak in his assessment of humankind: "Everything that exists is born without a reason, prolongs itself out of weakness, and dies by chance."[10] Also last century, zoologist Desmond Morris described us as "naked apes."[11] We have bigger brains than other primates but far less hair, he argued. This century, noted scientific thinker Richard Dawkins argues that human beings are the products of a blind evolutionary process and are soft tissue packages through which the selfish gene replicates itself. In an interview he stated that "living organisms and their bodies are best seen as machines programmed by the genes to propagate those very same genes."[12] Jordan Peterson captures the anxiety of many when he writes, "It's easy for human beings to think of themselves as trivial specs on a trivial spec out of some misbegotten hellhole-end-of-the-galaxy among hundreds of galaxies."[13]

The book that understands me tells a very different story. Yes, we are creatures just as other animals are. Creatures are finite, limited. Granted. But there is a special descriptor used of us in the earliest part of the Bible. We are made in the image of God, both male and female. We are precious. That's why to take a human life is a very serious moral matter. To take a human life could mean your own life is forfeited (e.g., in the case of premeditated murder). However, we are also now fallen creatures living in a ruptured relationship with our Creator. Augustine in late antiquity wrote of the fall of humankind.[14] Jacques Ellul in the twentieth century wrote of the rupture of our relationship with God, with each other and with the environment.[15]

What we think we are and how we value human life are linked. Quaker philosopher Elton Trueblood saw the linkage and its implications. He wrote:

> A quarter of a century ago [1944] a few of us began to say that faith in the possibility of a cut-flower civilization is a faith which is bound to fail. What we meant was that it is impossible to sustain certain elements of human dignity, once these have been severed from their cultural roots. The sorrowful fact is that, while the cut flowers seem to go on living and may even exhibit some brightness for a while, they cannot do so permanently, for they will eventually wither and be discarded. The historical truth is that the chief sources of the concepts of the dignity of the individual and equality before the law are found in the Biblical heritage. Apart from the fundamental convictions of that heritage, symbolized by the idea that every man is made in the image of God, there is no adequate reason for accepting the concepts mentioned. Since human beings are often far from admirable in their actual behavior, man's dignity is fundamentally derivative in nature.[16]

The cut flower analogy is a startling one. Who hasn't seen a bunch of flowers left too long in the bowl? The petals turn brown and start falling off. The stems start to droop. Not a pretty sight.

Ideas matter. If I see other human beings as cosmic accidents, my valuation of them, and of myself, shows it. But if I see both them and me as being in the image of God, it makes a difference. Atheistic philosopher Jean Paul Sartre shows us the difference when he describes humanity in these terms: "Man is a useless passion. It is meaningless that we live and it is meaningless that we die."[17] Secular ethicist Peter Singer argues for a similar view, when he maintains that being human gives no superior moral status and that human beings are not all equal in moral value. He writes:

> Many people believe that all human life is of equal value. Most of them also believe that all human beings have a moral status superior to that of nonhuman animals. But how are these beliefs to be defended? The mere difference of species cannot in itself determine moral status. The most obvious candidate for regarding human beings as having a higher moral status than animals is the superior cognitive capacity of humans. People with profound mental retardation pose a problem for this set of beliefs, because their cognitive capacities are not superior to those of many animals. I argue that we should drop the belief in the equal value of human life, replacing it with a graduated view that applies to animals as well as to humans.[18]

Singer writes as a naturalistic thinker. Material reality is the sum total of what is. Religious faith has no place in his universe, and it shows.

Interestingly, however, when Peter Singer's own mother developed dementia he found it hard to live by his philosophy. His philosophy allows for the euthanizing of dementia sufferers. His rationale for this is provided by the need to use limited resources in the best way possible. But as Mark Coffey points out:

> In reply to questions about the tens of thousands of dollars spent by Singer in providing private health care for his mother, Singer acknowledges that his own criteria—by which she is no longer a person and would suffer no wrong, indeed may be treated more compassionately, were she killed—determine that the money could probably be put to better use, yet he comments "[I]t is more difficult than I thought before, because it is different when it is your mother."[19]

It is worth asking of any philosophy not only is it thinkable but is it also livable? A philosophy may be internally consistent and coherent but can it be lived out as though it were true? In the end Singer could not live his philosophy.[20]

Rooted in his Christian faith, Martin Luther King Jr. had a very different view than that of Sartre and Singer:

> You see the founding fathers were really influenced by the Bible. The whole concept of the imago Dei ... is the idea that all men have something within them that God injected. Not that they have substantial unity with God, but that every man has a capacity to have fellowship with God. And this gives him uniqueness. ... There are no gradations in the image of God. Every man from a treble white to a bass black is significant on God's keyboard, precisely because every man is made in the image of God. One day we will learn that. We will know one day that God made us to live together as brothers and to respect the dignity and worth of every man. This is why we must fight segregation with all of our non-violent might.[21]

For King these were not merely ideas but grounds for action as can be seen in his non-violent protest rallies and marches. His belief in human value led him to protest discrimination and champion civil rights.

Medical doctor and academic John Wyatt provides an illuminating contrast between two views of humankind. The first he calls "Lego Kits." Think of the variety of things that can be made from Lego: boats, people, planes, houses, and so on. As Wyatt puts it, "We are free to be our own designers."[22] The natural order can be changed through the application of technology which is value free. The other view he terms "God's masterpieces." On this approach our embodiment is a gift from God. However, he argues, "The original masterpiece, created with such love and embodying such artistry, has become flawed, defaced, and contaminated."[23] The message of the Bible is that God's project is one of "art restoration." Jesus Christ plays the crucial role in the project. God's Son became human and rose in bodily form. The value of the human body is thus affirmed. Moreover, Wyatt argues, "In biblical thought, each human life has a unique dignity because of the divine image, therefore each life has an incalculable and incommensurable value."[24] As we have seen, it was this belief that animated Martin Luther King Jr. This same belief also energized Mother Teresa in her ministry to the dying poor of Calcutta. At her funeral it was rightly said, "The story of Mother Teresa's life is no mere humanitarian exploit, as she would be the first to declare. It is a story of biblical faith. It can only be explained as a proclamation of Jesus Christ by—in her own words— 'loving and serving Him in the distressing disguise of the poorest of the poor, both materially and spiritually, recognizing in them and restoring to them the image and likeness of God.'"[25]

We not only see ourselves afresh as to our value but we also see afresh what the human problematic is. We are paradoxical beings. Blaise Pascal captured the paradox well in one of his *pensées* ("thoughts"): "What sort of freak then is man! How novel, how monstrous, how chaotic, how paradoxical, how prodigious! Judge of all things, feeble earthworm, repository of truth, sink of doubt and error, glory and refuse of the universe."[26] He captures the human predicament another way when he writes: "All these examples of wretchedness prove his greatness. It is the wretchedness of a great lord, the wretchedness of a dispossessed king."[27] The apostle Paul put the issue in moral and religious terms when he wrote to Christians in Rome and summed up the human situation in these terms (Rom 3:22–23): "There is no difference between Jew and Gentile, for all have sinned and fall short of the glory of God."

We have defected from the God who made us. Self-absorption comes all too easily and with it the temptation to make everything about me.[28] A story I heard captures the point. Two people meet by accident on a street corner. They had been in high school together but had not seen each other for years. One got to talking and talked and talked. Talked about degrees done since high school, about marriages entered into and failed, talked about jobs and career path. The other person became restless and started shuffling their feet. Our talker noticed and said: "I have just talked on and on about me. How about I ask a question of you?" "Go ahead," the somewhat relieved other person said. "Wonderful," was the reply. "So let me ask: What do you think about me?"

The book that understands me knows my need for value and sees that I fall so far short of what I expect of others. I need forgiveness, and, as we saw before, the love of God has made that possible, according to this book, through what Christ did for me on the cross. God can break the cycle of toxic self-concern.[29]

Third, we see history afresh.

The big Bible story presents human history as a road with a beginning and an end. It is not like some Eastern religious views that see existence as an illusion and the key metaphor is not the road, but the wheel, a wheel endlessly rotating and going nowhere—an endless cycle that must be escaped. This has been called the wheel understanding of life. Lesslie Newbigin writes perceptively about the wheel view. He writes too from firsthand experience of decades spent in India and in dialogue with Hindu religious thinkers.

> The cycle of birth, growth, decay and death through which plants, animals, human beings and institutions all pass suggests the rotating wheel—ever in movement yet ever returning upon itself. The wheel offers a way to the center where all is still, and one can observe the ceaseless movement without being involved in it. There are many spokes connecting the circumference with the center. The wise man will not quarrel about which spoke should be chosen. Any one will do, provided it leads to the center. Dispute among the different "ways" of salvation is pointless; all that matters is that those who follow them should find their way to that timeless, motionless center where all is peace, and where one can understand all the endless movement and change which makes up human history—understand that it goes nowhere and means nothing.[30]

This is clearly a pessimistic worldview. History, and human life with it, are meaningless.

Newbigin also writes with great insight into another way to construe reality. This he calls the road view. The biblical understanding of history exemplifies this view. He writes:

> The other symbol is the road. History is a journey, a pilgrimage. We do not yet see the goal, but we believe in it and seek it. The movement in which we are involved is not meaningless movement; it is movement towards a goal. The goal, the ultimate resting-place, the experience of coherence and harmony, is not to be had save at the end of the road. The perfect goal is not a timeless reality hidden now behind the multiplicity and change which we experience; it is yet to be achieved; it lies at the end of the road.[31]

The wheel and the road constitute "the great divide" in world religions, according to Newbigin.[32]

The Bible understands my need for meaning, my need to understand the human story as meaningful and not an exercise in futility. How different to Shakespeare's *Macbeth*: "Life's but a walking shadow, a poor player / That struts and frets his hour upon the stage / And then is heard no more. It is a tale / Told by an idiot, full of sound and fury, / Signifying nothing."[33]

Fourth, we see the present afresh.

A year ago I was in beautiful part of Sydney, Australia, called the Northern Beaches. Spectacular in every way: sun, sand and surf. I had a conversation with a local pastor and I was shocked to learn of the epidemic of youth suicides in this gorgeous setting—young people who do not know why life is worth living. French writer Antoine de Saint-Exupéry wrote: "Prison is not a mere physical horror. It is using a pickaxe to no purpose that makes a prison." But where can purpose be found?

The book that understands me knows of my need for purpose. Caring is that purpose and it takes three forms. First, if the Bible is to be believed, humankind has a mandate to care for the earth. The metaphor that captures this idea is that of steward. A steward has a duty of care. In stewardship under God, we human beings have an obligation to carry out what has been termed "creation care." This is the creation mandate. The notion that as superior animals we are free to exploit nature for any purpose that gives pleasure or profit is far from the idea of creation care. There can be a religious expression of this that trades on the image of God phrase found in the Bible.[34] Second, we are to care for people. According to the book that understands me, that includes not only my neighbor but even my enemy. This is the moral mandate. Last, we are to care about God. That caring shows itself in worship. This is the worship mandate. Worship is a practice that takes us out of ourselves and our self-preoccupations to center on another. In fact, all three mandates are expressed in practices that center not on ourselves but look outwards. To use spatial ideas: downward to the earth, around us toward other people, and upwards to God.

The Bible understands my need for purpose, for things to do. Friedrich Nietzsche was right: "He who has a why to live for can bear almost any how."[35] Psychotherapist Jordan Peterson acknowledges the same need when he writes, "The nobler the aim, the better the life."[36]

Fifth, we see the future afresh.

It was a sobering experience meeting an elderly woman in the nursing home. She was the mother of the husband of my Jewish cousin. She rolled up her sleeve and showed me the number tattooed on her forearm. She had been in a Nazi concentration camp but had somehow survived. Psychotherapist Viktor Frankl had also experienced the hell of a concentration camp and made this observation: Those prisoners who had hope survived. Those who didn't, perished. He expressed it this way: "The prisoner who had lost faith in the future—his future—was doomed."[37]

Science has blessed us with so much to enjoy and benefit from. Without medical science and the technology that goes with it I would be facing blindness because of cataracts growing in both eyes. Surgery has made all the difference. The big scientific picture, however, provides little comfort. Philosopher Bertrand Russell was unflinching in facing that lack of comfort and his famous words show it. Although he wrote these words over a century ago, they are still chilling:

> Such, in outline, but even more purposeless, more void of meaning, is the world which Science presents for our belief. Amid such a world, if anywhere, our ideals henceforward must find a home. That Man is the product of causes which had no prevision of the end they were achieving; that his origin, his growth, his hopes and fears, his loves and his beliefs, are but the outcome of accidental collocations of atoms; that no fire, no heroism, no intensity of thought and feeling, can preserve an individual life beyond the grave; that all the labours of the ages, all the devotion, all the inspiration, all the noonday brightness of human genius, are destined to extinction in the vast death of the solar system, and that the whole temple of Man's achievement must inevitably be buried beneath the debris of a universe in ruins—all these things, if not quite beyond dispute, are yet so nearly certain, that no philosophy which rejects them can hope to stand.[38]

Russell concludes his essay with this disturbing thought: "Only within the scaffolding of these truths, only on the firm foundation of unyielding despair, can the soul's habitation henceforth be safely built."[39]

In contrast to Russell's pessimism, as we have seen, there is a road. At least that's the claim. History has a plotline that according to the Bible moves from creation through the fall of humankind to its rescue and, in the final act, the restoration of the entire created order. But to be part of that restoration is a matter of embracing an invitation. Invited to what? The answer is a "whom" not a "what." I am invited to trust another. Insight is all well and good. But relationships are the key to human joy. I can love knowledge, but it can't love me. Persons love. In the pages of the Bible I meet a person who loves me.

The great philosopher of the Enlightenment, Immanuel Kant, argued that there are three big questions in life: What can I know? What ought I to do? For what may I hope?[40] With regard to his last question, the Bible understands my need for hope.

4

REASON AND ITS LIMITATIONS

TO ENCOURAGE TRUST in the Bible as the book that understands us may seem to some an invitation to folly. Isn't it asking for a sacrifice of the intellect? By "intellect" usually it is reason that is meant. Here we need some clear thinking. Reason does not exist apart from persons. Persons reason. By that I mean they mount arguments, offer refutations, marshal evidence for or against a claim to truth.

A figure from the past, Martin Luther, has some wise analysis to offer with regard to the human capacity to reason. He viewed reality in terms of a heavenly kingdom and an earthly one. Carefully understood, reason can operate usefully in both. Luther used three categories in his analysis. First, there is the natural or productive reasoning that is used to do things like cobble shoes. This is reason at work in the earthly kingdom. Then there is faithful reasoning that serves God with the mind. This is reason in serving mode in the heavenly kingdom. Lastly, however, there is a use of reasoning that Luther rejected. For him this was unfaithful reason or the devil's whore (Frau Hülda).[41] This use of reasoning is in evidence when the human capacity to reason is wedded to an attitude of hostility and presumption toward God.[42]

The human ability to reason is not an attitude-free zone.

5

AN EXAMINED FAITH

ONE OF THE earliest philosophical texts that I studied came from ancient Greece. It was Socrates's *Apology*. He was on trial before his fellow Athenian citizens for allegedly corrupting the city's youth. In making his defense, Socrates uttered a famous idea that the unexamined life is not worth living.[43] Socrates knew the power of asking awkward questions. Examination is a question-asking enterprise.

I became a follower of Jesus in my late teens with no real knowledge of the Bible so I had many, many questions. In the church I started to attend I asked my questions and was told not to ask questions but believe. I soon came to the view that an unexamined faith, just like an unexamined life, is not worth having. Happily I found books and people with satisfying answers for that stage of my life. More importantly, I found the Bible full of arguments addressed to my reason.

The claim that Jesus rose bodily from the dead as portrayed in the New Testament part of the Bible illustrates what I mean. It seems that some in the early church had their doubts about the resurrection, especially at Corinth in ancient Greece. So the apostle Paul needed to respond. In a letter he sent to the church there, he wrote:

> Now, brothers and sisters, I want to remind you of the gospel I preached to you, which you received and on which you have taken your stand. By this gospel you are saved, if you hold firmly to the word I preached to you. Otherwise, you have believed in vain.
>
> For what I received I passed on to you as of first importance: that Christ died for our sins according to the Scriptures, that he was buried, that he was raised on the third day according to the Scriptures, and that he appeared to Cephas and then to the Twelve. After that, he appeared to more than five hundred of the brothers and sisters at the same time, most of whom are still living, though some have fallen asleep. Then he appeared to James, then to all the apostles, and last of all he appeared to me also, as to one abnormally born.
>
> For I am the least of the apostles and do not even deserve to be called an apostle, because I persecuted the church of God. But by the grace of God I am what I am, and his grace to me was not without effect. No, I worked harder than all of them—yet not I, but the grace of God that was with me. Whether, then, it is I or they, this is what we preach, and this is what you believed. (1 Cor 15:1–11)

What strikes me about Paul's approach is that it appeals to reason through the presentation of evidence. It is a presentation worth closer inspection.

In form, Paul's argument is a cumulative one. First, Paul points out that his message was not one invented by him. He is passing on the message—the gospel (news) he received from others. Second, he claims that the Old Testament Scriptures tell the same story. He does not cite any particular part of the Old Testament. That may be because these Corinthian Christians knew already what he taught as he had dealings with them in the past. Third, the risen Christ appeared to real people with real names: Cephas (a.k.a. Peter), and other apostles (the Twelve). Indeed, Christ appeared to over five hundred followers in one event, most of them still alive at the time of writing. (The implication is that this claim can be checked out.) He also appeared to James who was Jesus' skeptical brother. To cap it off, Paul cites his own firsthand experience of the risen Christ. Significantly, during the time leading up to his conversion, he was opposed to all that Jesus and his followers stood for.

Paul's argument does not end there. He entertains the idea that he has got it all wrong in these claims and if so, what would follow. He presents what could be described as the logic of the alternative which takes the form of a number of step syllogisms (the "if … then" arguments).

> But if it is preached that Christ has been raised from the dead, how can some of you say that there is no resurrection of the dead? If there is no resurrection of the dead, then not even Christ has been raised.

> And if Christ has not been raised, our preaching is useless and so is your faith. More than that, we are then found to be false witnesses about God, for we have testified about God that he raised Christ from the dead. But he did not raise him if in fact the dead are not raised. For if the dead are not raised, then Christ has not been raised either. And if Christ has not been raised, your faith is futile; you are still in your sins. Then those also who have fallen asleep in Christ are lost. If only for this life we have hope in Christ, we are of all people most to be pitied. But Christ has indeed been raised from the dead, the firstfruits of those who have fallen asleep. (1 Cor 15:12–20)

Paul imagines what reality would look like if Christ had not triumphed over death. Faith would be useless. Faith in a dead messiah is pointless. Worse still, Paul would be a misleading preacher who misrepresented God. Moreover, the problem of our wrong-doing, our sin, would remain unaddressed. Anyone believing this stuff is to be pitied. The very fact that Paul can envisage an alternative to Christ actually rising from the dead ought to caution anyone suggesting that the apostle was a one-eyed fanatic for his faith. My experience of the ideologically driven is that there are no alternatives to the platform they advocate.

What is clear from this part of the New Testament is that people aren't told simply to believe without questioning. Paul's readers are not called to embrace an unexamined faith. Paul is not the only writer in the New Testament who sees the need for argument. This is what Peter wrote to some Christians living in what is now modern Turkey:

> Who is going to harm you if you are eager to do good? But even if you should suffer for what is right, you are blessed. "Do not fear their threats; do not be frightened." But in your hearts revere Christ as Lord. Always be prepared to give an answer [defense] to everyone who asks you to give the reason for the hope that you have. But do this with gentleness and respect, keeping a clear conscience, so that those who speak maliciously against your good behavior in Christ may be ashamed of their slander. For it is better, if it is God's will, to suffer for doing good than for doing evil. (1 Pet 3:13–17)

Peter knew that his readers were facing hostility from their neighbors and needed to know how to conduct themselves under pressure. He reminds his readers of the importance of lifestyle ("eager to do good"), and insists that tone is important ("gentleness and respect"). Live down criticism with a clear conscience. Doing evil is a no-no. Importantly, be prepared to mount a defense of your faith, and "give the reason for the hope that you have." To make a defense (literally "apology") in this sense and to give the reason (*logos*) for one's hope is an appeal to the mind.

The book that understands me recognizes my need for argument and reasons.

6

A SECULARIST WITH QUESTIONS

ROSARIA CHAMPAGNE BUTTERFIELD has an interesting story to tell. She says, "As a leftist lesbian professor, I despised Christians. Then I somehow became one."[44] She was a postmodern intellectual and an expert in queer studies. Her worldview was materialist, not supernaturalist. She started doing research on the Religious Right and "their politics of hate" as she put it. To do this properly she knew she needed to read the Bible for herself.

She was a professor of English at a secular university and as a trained academic she knew how to research with integrity. In her own words:

> I started reading the Bible. I read the way a glutton devours. I read it many times that first year in multiple translations. At a dinner gathering my partner and I were hosting, my transgendered friend J cornered me in the kitchen. She put her large hand over mine. "This Bible reading is changing you, Rosaria," she warned.

Fresh questions came to her mind:

> With tremors, I whispered, "J, what if it is true? What if Jesus is a real and risen Lord? What if we are all in trouble?"

> I continued reading the Bible, all the while fighting the idea that it was inspired. But the Bible got to be bigger inside me than I. It overflowed into my world.[45]

She recounts:

> When I started to read the Bible it was to critique it, embarking on a research project on the Religious Right and their hatred against queers, or, at the time, people like me. But the Bible was getting under my skin. Hours each day I poured over this text, arguing at first, then contemplating, and eventually surrendering. Three principles became insurmountable on my own terms: the trinitarian God's goodness, the trinitarian God's holiness, and the authority of Scripture.[46]

Admirably she began reading the Bible as matter of intellectual honesty. If you are going to critique X then get to know as much as you can about X. Over time the Bible itself overcame her resistance to it. She put it in this way: "Oh, yes. The Bible is an amazing book, and I had never read it. I was more than happy to criticize a book I'd never read. I'm a bookish kind of gal, and the Bible really gets inside of you. And it made me confront some really haunting things. It made me face a whole category of sin—both mine and other people's."[47]

Now having read thus far you may be someone who knows the kind of resistance that Butterfield knew. If so ask yourself two key questions about any resistance you find within yourself: Is the problem one of understanding or is it one of life? I recall talking to an academic at a state university who had asked me for some literature about the historicity of Jesus. He returned the books and said that the evidence was surprisingly good. He asked that if the evidence were as good as it appears to be why more people didn't believe it. I replied that many people just don't know how good it is.

The second question to ask as you read the Bible is, How would my life change if I embraced what it is saying? Resistance may come because the answer would be uncomfortable. I had a remarkable experience of seeing how a problem in life led to a rejection of the Bible's invitation. It was while I was an undergraduate. I was studying for a liberal arts degree. A number of high school friends and I found ourselves in the same university. Over a number of months I shared with my friend books giving evidence and arguments to support Christianity's truth claims, especially about Jesus. My friend was studying science with a view to doing medicine. After some six months, he shared that be believed that Jesus was the Son of God and had risen from the dead. I was thrilled and said how wonderful that he was now a Christian. But no, he said, he wasn't. He explained to me that if he became a Christian, God might want him to give up his pursuit of medicine and become a missionary. (To this day I am not sure why he thought that.) For him, the problem was a possible change in his life's direction.

The book that understands me calls upon me to change. Some things cannot be seen without a change in position. For a time I lived in Cambridge in England. Nearby is Ely Cathedral. The cathedral is over a thousand years old and dominates the landscape, so much so it is locally referred to as "the ship of the fens." Looking from the outside it can seem dull in color. But step inside on a sunny day and the cathedral is full of beautiful light and the stained glass windows are alive. A change of position makes all the difference. My friend was not prepared to step inside.[48]

7

AND YET QUESTIONS PERSIST

OVER THE YEARS I have found many answers to my questions in the Bible's pages. That does not mean, however, that questions do not persist. The fact of evil in our world continues to perplex me, especially where children are involved. That's where the AFL box comes into play. AFL stands for Awaiting Further Light.[49]

For many years, I had this question in my AFL box: Why is the universe so big if, according to the Bible, the earth is where the action is to be found? After all, Christians claim that God became incarnate (i.e. human without ceasing to be God) on this planet which is part of only one solar system which in turn is part of only one galaxy, the Milky Way, which itself is an estimated 100 million light-years across. Scientist Caitlin Casey captures the point well: "It's rather humbling. Astronomy has taught us that we're not the centre of the Universe, we're not even at the centre of our Solar System or at the centre of our galaxy."[50]

After teaching philosophy for a number of years, I came up with one possible answer. There are different kinds of value. Truth is an intellectual value. Goodness is a moral value. Beauty is an aesthetic value. Perhaps when the Bible relates how God describes the various aspects of creation as "good," there is an aesthetic dimension to the idea. In other words, God enjoys the beauty of the vast universe of which our planet is a tiny part. After all, I enjoy the beauty of the images of outer space I see, so why not God who is a person too?

Some years later, I found myself leading a seminar at Monash University in Australia with John Polkinghorne, who is both a scientist and a theologian by training. For years he was a professor of mathematical physics at the University of Cambridge. He answered the question in a different but complementary way. He argued that the minerals that make up the human body were forged in the stars and that without a universe the size that we conjecture it to be, human beings would not be here. I now had two answers to my questions whereas for a number of years I had none.

So don't be surprised if you have questions. Don't be surprised that some questions may take years before a satisfactory answer comes. Don't be surprised if some questions are not answered at all. The fact is that the Bible does not cover every imaginable topic. It tells us as much. Here is what Moses told Israel back in the day. The setting is a plain just outside the land of promise: Moses is preaching and here is the climax (Deut 29:29): "The secret things belong to the LORD our God, but the things revealed belong to us and to our children forever, that we may follow all the words of this law." There are two categories on view: secret things and revealed things. Moreover, the revealed things have to do with the practice of life for which we need law, which in the context means guidance or instruction.

Of course, there is a place for theory formation and speculation. I have a theory as to why an all good, all wise and all powerful God has allowed evil to intrude into creation. The fact of the matter is that the Bible is non-postulation on this and many other subjects. It offers no theories as to the essences of things. The interest of Scripture is relation: my relation to God, my relation to you and my relation to nature.

8

ACQUIRING A TASTE

AT ONE STAGE in my life I gave the Christians I knew a hard time. I challenged them about myths and legends in the Bible. The problem was that I had never even opened a Bible. That did not stop me. I was using newspaper and magazine articles as my sources. It seems that just about every Christmas and Easter there are stories questioning the truth of Christian claims about Jesus. These were the stories I used to challenge the Christians I knew. Then I read it for myself. I have since become an avid Bible reader. I also learned to pray before I read that God would give me understanding and affection for what I was reading. Strikingly some of the Bible writers describe revelation from God as a delicious delicacy to be eaten. The Old Testament psalmist compares that revelatory word to honey (Ps 119:103).

Of course, there were puzzling things that I read or heard. I remember early on sitting in church and hearing about how Israelite priests carried the ark across the River Jordan. Nonsense, I thought. How could anyone carry Noah's ark like that? I soon learned that in the Bible the word "ark" could refer to a very different object. The Ark of the Covenant was a box in which certain sacred objects were housed like the Ten Commandments on tablets of stone. It could be carried. (If only I had seen Stephen Spielberg's, *Raiders of the Lost Ark*—but that came later.) At times, I needed to consult others to truly understand what I was reading or hearing. Books helped immensely. Good preaching that explained the Bible with care and intelligence also helped me greatly. So to develop a wise reading strategy we need to be prepared to consult others when necessary.

Coming from Australia to live in the United States, I found my first American Thanksgiving holiday was a new cultural experience. For Americans, this is a great family reconnection time. Now eating is an intimate activity. It requires engagement. Simply sitting at a table is not enough to be fed. To participate in Thanksgiving, you can't simply look at the food. The knife must be taken up and the fork used. Eating with a knife and fork takes time to learn. We start learning to do so when we are very young. As an adult I have had that same need for time to learn how to use chopsticks. So what about the skills needed to be a wise reader and what do we read first? I recommend beginning with the Gospel of John in modern English.[51] This gospel confronts us with the magnetic figure of Jesus and has proved transformative in the experience of many.[52] The language is simple; the ideas in it are profound. I also recommend adopting a well-thought-out reading strategy. In this regard, I like the Swedish Bible study method.[53] If you find your mind enlightened as you read use a pencil to draw a candle or a light bulb next to the text. Or if have downloaded the gospel then use words in a comment space to do so. If the text strikes your conscience in some way and challenges you to change your attitudes or behavior then draw an arrow in the text.[54] Don't expect every text or aspect of the text to make perfect sense on first reading. If puzzled, draw a question mark. Do research to seek an answer to your question.[55] Ask around. Pray for clarity.

Since I have mentioned John's Gospel let me use it to illustrate what these tools look like in action. The narrative climaxes with this editorial comment: "Jesus performed many other signs in the presence of his disciples, which are not recorded in this book. But these are written that you may believe that Jesus is the Messiah, the Son of God, and that by believing you may have life in his name" (John 20:30–31). For me a lightbulb is the reference to the other signs not recorded. I learn from this that this foundational New Testament writing is highly selective. I should not expect it to be able to answer all the questions about Jesus that I might have. As for the arrow targeting my conscience, I cannot think of any issue of conscience that the statement arouses in me. What this illustrates is that not every tool will be relevant every time. Questions abound. What is a "sign"? What do those titles ascribed to Jesus mean? What is the "life" referred to and how does this life come through a name?

Everyone today seems in such a hurry, don't they? The appeal of the instant fix is pervasive. Speed dating, speed with everything (except the Grammy Awards). However, worthwhile relationships take time. This is true at the personal level with friends. That's why some people are only acquaintances or work colleagues. It is also true in other areas of life. It takes a while to deeply appreciate art or music. As John Piper argues, all of us stand in some relationship to the Bible.[56] It may be we have been raised to trust it like Piper or to be skeptical like I was. Being drawn into the Bible's vista too takes time. It was only over time that I came to appreciate that this book really understands me.

CONCLUSION

LIFE POSES QUESTIONS. Why am I here? Who or what am I? Why do I hurt those who love me? Why do I fall short of who I should be? Is this life all there is? How can I get perspective on such questions in the quest to understand? In Chicago, where I live, stands one of America's tallest buildings. The Willis Tower is 110 stories and 1,729 feet to its tip. From its Skydeck on the 103rd floor I can see vast tracts of Chicago. I can see the northern, western, and southern suburbs, and I can see magnificent Lake Michigan. The tower gives me a vantage point. The Bible provides me with a vantage point and opens up a vista. It gives me perspective. Reading its pages helps me to see so much that I would not otherwise see. In fact in its pages I have found a book that understands me. It understands my need for purpose in life, a noble aim. It understands my need for value. It understands my need for realism about human behavior: the good and the bad. It understands my need for hope. It understands my need to make sense of things. Embracing such understanding requires an open mind, but not an empty head. This book understands my need for evidence and argument, not blind belief. However, perspective and understanding only take us so far. The book not only informs. The book offers an invitation to embrace a relationship. It reveals a person, a person worthy of our trust.

Acknowledgments

THE SERIES Questions for Restless Minds is produced by the Christ on Campus Initiative, under the stewardship of the editorial board of D. A. Carson (senior editor), Douglas Sweeney, Graham Cole, Dana Harris, Thomas McCall, Geoffrey Fulkerson, and Scott Manetsch. The editorial board recognizes with gratitude the many outstanding evangelical authors who have contributed to this series, as well as the sponsorship of Trinity Evangelical Divinity School (Deerfield, Illinois), and the financial support of the MAC Foundation and the Carl F. H. Henry Center for Theological Understanding. The editors also wish to thank Christopher Gow, who created the study questions accompanying each book, and Todd Hains, our editor at Lexham Press. May God alone receive the glory for this endeavor!

Study Guide Questions

1. What do you think Cole means when he says that the Bible is a book that "understands" us? Can you think of a moment or a season of life when you felt "understood" by the Bible?
2. How would you describe the meaning and importance of the Bible's teaching that humans are "made in the image of God"?
3. Cole says that the Bible gives us insight into God, ourselves, history, the present, and the future. Were any of these categories new or surprising to you?
4. How does Cole summarize the Bible's insight on each of these topics? Is there anything you would add or change?
5. What are some questions that you have or areas of your faith that are AFL (Awaiting Further Light)?

6. Can you identify any areas of resistance to God in your heart/mind/life?

    a. Is the problem one of understanding or of life?

    b. How would your life change if you wholeheartedly embraced the Bible's teaching?

7. Before concluding, Cole says "the interest of Scripture is relation" (55). What do you think about this? Does this assertion resonate with the way you read the Bible? Why/why not? How could you engage Scripture in a way that is primarily interested in relation?

For Further Reading

Blomberg, Craig L. *Who Is Jesus of Nazareth?* Lexham Press, 2021.

New Testament scholar Blomberg tackles the key question in this book. The Bible would not be worth reading if it is wrong in its claims about its central character, Jesus. Blomberg gives arguments for confidence.

Blowes, Peter. "The Swedish Method," http://matthiasmedia.com/briefing/2009/01/the-swedish-method/.

In this article Blowes writes out of his intercultural experience in Argentina where he worked for nineteen years. He explains the message, gives its theological underpinnings, points out its adaptability to different contexts and how it may be deepened. For the Gospel of John online in modern translation, see https://www.biblegateway.com/passage/?search=John+1&version=NIV.

Butterfield, Rosaria Champagne. "My Train Wreck Conversion," http://www.christianitytoday.com/ct/2013/january-february/my-train-wreck-conversion.html?start=1.

Butterfield also undertook a journey: from lesbian activist to a pastor's wife. She has written at length about her journey in *The Secret Thoughts of an Unlikely Convert: An English Professor's Journey into the Christian Faith* (Crown and Covenant, 2012).

——, "You are What—and How—You Read," https://www.thegospelcoalition.org/article/you-are-whatand-howyou-read/.

Butterfield has a keen interest in how people read, as she believes that reading can shape character.

Cailliet, Émile. *Journey into Light*. Zondervan, 1968.

The journey of which Cailliet speaks is from naturalism to a vibrant Christian faith and from France to the United States. Of particular interest is the role the Bible played in that journey.

Carson, D. A., ed. *NIV Zondervan Study Bible*. Zondervan, 2015.

Over sixty scholars contributed to this volume with 28 articles and some 20,000 study notes.

Kilner, John F., ed. *Why People Matter: A Christian Engagement with Rival Views of Human Significance*. Baker Academic, 2017.

How one values oneself and others is tied to how humankind is viewed. This book critically explores a number of views: utilitarianism, collectivism, individualism, naturalism and the transhuman option. It argues that "a biblically grounded Christian outlook" provides "the best basis for affirming human significance—not grounded in humanity or science but in God and God's design for humans" (14). Nearly every chapter ends with an annotated bibliography.

Piper, John. *A Peculiar Glory: How the Christian Scriptures Reveal Their Complete Truthfulness*. Crossway, 2016.

Piper's book is more than autobiography. He covers many questions that an appeal to the Bible beg. For example, four questions in particular drive the book: What books and words make up the Christian Scriptures? What do the Christian Scriptures claim for themselves? How can we know the Christian Scriptures are true? How are the Christian Scriptures confirmed by the peculiar glory of God?

Notes

1. The idea of a book that understands us is not a strange one. A bookstore has plenty of books that seek to help us understand ourselves to greater or lesser degrees. I think of books about Myers-Briggs Personality Types or the Enneagram. Given the title, this essay will have autobiographical aspects to it as well as reflect my interests in culture, literature, philosophy, and theology.
2. Émile Cailliet, *Journey into Light* (Zondervan: 1968), 16.
3. Cailliet, *Journey into Light*, 16.
4. Cailliet, *Journey into Light*, 16.
5. Cailliet, *Journey into Light*, 17. Original italics.
6. Cailliet, *Journey into Light*, 18.
7. John Piper, *A Peculiar Glory: How the Christian Scriptures Reveal Their Complete Truthfulness* (Crossway, 2016), 26–27. Original emphases. Piper explains what he means by the phrase "the glory of God" in the following way: "Close to the heart of what makes the glory of God is the way his maj-

esty and his meekness combine," 217. That combination is seen in Jesus Christ, 225–26.

8. It may seem strange to treat the sixty-six books that make up the Bible in such a unified way. But Christians believe that behind the many authors writing over many centuries the supreme author was God himself. Moreover the Bible writers themselves can personify the Bible of their own day in such unified terms. Paul the apostle did so in writing to Christians in ancient Galatia (Gal 3:8): "Scripture foresaw that God would justify the Gentiles by faith, and announced the gospel in advance to Abraham: 'All nations will be blessed through you.'" Even secular thinker and professor of psychology Jordan Peterson is astonished that the collection of books that make up the Bible "has a story." In fact, he describes the Bible as "the world's first hyperlinked text" with some "65 thousand cross-references." See Jordan Peterson, "Biblical Series 1: Introduction to the Idea of God," https://www.jordanbpeterson.com/transcripts/biblical-series-i.
9. John Calvin, *Institutes of the Christian Religion,* 1.6.1.
10. Jean Paul Sartre quoted in Richard Askay and Jensen Farquhar, *Apprehending the Inaccessible: Freudian Psychoanalysis and Existential Phenomenology* (Northwestern University Press, 1960), 230.
11. Desmond Morris, *The Naked Ape: The Controversial Classic* (Random House, 1967).

12. Interview with Richard Dawkins, "Faith and Reason," *PBS*, http://www.pbs.org/faithandreason/transcript/dawk-frame.html. It is important to note that Dawkins is describing humankind as he sees it and not advocating a morality of selfishness. See Richard Dawkins, *The Selfish Gene* (Oxford University Press, 1989), 4–5, 267.
13. Peterson, "Biblical Series 1: Introduction to the Idea of God." Peterson himself thinks that this view is mistaken. The phenomenon of human consciousness, he argues, suggests that we are more than specs. Renowned theoretical physicist Stephen Hawkings makes a similar point: "We are just an advanced breed of monkeys on a minor planet of a very average star. But we can understand the universe. That makes us something very special," quoted in Onyanga-Omara, "Stephen Hawkings memorable quotes," *USA Today*, March 14, 2018, https://www.usatoday.com/story/news/world/2018/03/14/stephen-hawking-quotations/423145002/.
14. Augustine, *The City of God*, Book 14, Chapter 11, https://www.ccel.org/ccel/schaff/npnf102.iv.XIV.11.html.
15. Andrew Goddard, "Jacques Ellul's Theological Writings," International Jacques Ellul Society, https://ellul.org/themes/theme-ellul-and-theological-writings/.

16. Elton Trueblood, *A Place to Stand* (Harper & Row, 1969), 14–15.
17. Jean-Paul Sartre, Goodreads.com, https://www.goodreads.com/quotes/7285836-man-is-a-useless-passion-it-is-meaningless-that-we. Also see Jean-Paul Sartre, *Being and Nothingness*, trans. Hazel E. Barnes (Washington Square, 1984), 784.
18. Peter Singer, "Speciesism and Moral Status," http://www.oswego.edu/~delancey/Singer.pdf.
19. Mark Coffey, "Ten Reasons Why I Love/Hate Peter Singer," *Philosophy Now*, January/February 2007, https://philosophynow.org/issues/59/Ten_Reasons_Why_I_Love_Hate_Peter_Singer.
20. To think clearly needs criteria. Three in particular come to mind. Is the view logical? That is to say, can you consistently think it through without falling into contradiction or incoherence? This is the logical adequacy criterion. Put another way, is this view thinkable? Another one is to ask, "Can you live as though your view is true to reality?" This is the existential adequacy criterion. Put another way: Is this view livable? This is the criterion that Singer's care for his mother falls foul of. For the Christian, a third question to ask is whether a view is scriptural. That is to say, is it found commended in the Bible or consistent with what is commended in the Bible? This might be called the scriptural adequacy criterion.

21. Martin Luther King Jr., Sermon, Ebenezer Baptist Church. Quote found in Keller, *Generous Justice: How God's Grace Makes Us Just* (Penguin Books, 2012), 86–87. In contrast, Peter Singer explicitly rejects any idea of human beings as made in the image of God. See note 34.
22. John Wyatt, *Matters of Life and Death: Human Dilemmas in the Light of the Christian Faith*, fully revised (IVP, 2009), 98. He sees the Lego Kit view as an outworking of the Enlightenment philosophy of the eighteenth century.
23. Wyatt, *Matters of Life and Death*, 98–99.
24. Wyatt, *Matters of Life and Death*, 60.
25. Cardinal Angelo Sodano, "Homily of the Funeral Mass for Mother Teresa of Calcutta," Mother Teresa Center, September 13, 1997, http://www.motherteresa.org/yearoffaith/MT.html. Sodano, the Vatican's secretary of state, was Pope John Paul II's personal representative at the service. The Mother Teresa quote Sodano references is from *Constitutions of the Missionaries of Charity*, 1.1)
26. Blaise Pascal, *Pascal Pensées*, revised edition, trans. A. J. Krailsheimer (Penguin, 1972), 34.
27. Pascal, *Pascal Pensées*, 29.
28. I don't mean "narcissism" in a technical sense of a personality disorder. Rather, I am using the word in the more general sense of excessive self-concern or egocentrism. See Merriam-Webster.com Dictio-

nary, s.v. "narcissistic," https://www.merriam-webster.com/dictionary/narcissistic.

29. I say "*toxic* self-concern" because there is a self-care that is entirely appropriate.
30. As Lesslie Newbigin, drawing on Nicol McNicol argued. See Paul Weston, Lesslie Newbigin, *Missionary Theologian: A Reader* (Eerdmans, 2006), 55.
31. Weston, Newbigin, *Missionary Theologian,* 55.
32. Weston, Newbigin, *Missionary Theologian,* 55.
33. William Shakespeare, *Macbeth*, 5.5.24–28.
34. As such some argue that the exploitation, rather than the intelligent use, of natural resources is a duty. The outcome of such an understanding can be dead rivers and barren landscape. Peter Singer is rightly critical of such an attitude. Even so his exposition of Christianity borders on caricature. See my chapter "Singer on Christianity: Characterized or Caricatured," in *Rethinking Peter Singer: A Christian Critique*, ed. Gordon Preece (IVP, 2002), 95–105.
35. Friedrich Nietzsche, Goodreads.com, https://www.goodreads.com/quotes/137-he-who-has-a-why-to-live-for-can-bear.
36. Peterson, "Biblical Series 1: Introduction to the Idea of God."
37. Victor Frankl, *Man's Search for Meaning* (Beacon, 2006), 74.
38. Bertrand Russell, "A Free Man's Worship," http://www.skeptic.ca/Bertrand_Russell_Collection.pdf.

39. Russell, "A Free Man's Worship." Contemporary scientific speculation about the future of the universe is hardly cheery. Journalist Jaime Trosper describes four scenarios: the Big Slurp, the Big Crunch, the Big Freeze, and the Big Rip. See "Four Ways That Our Universe Might End, According to Science," Futurism, March 3, 2014, https://futurism.com/four-ways-the-universe-could-end.
40. Immanuel Kant, *Critique of Pure Reason*, trans. and eds. Paul Guyer and Allen W. Wood (Cambridge University Press, 1998), http://strangebeautiful.com/other-texts/kant-first-critique-cambridge.pdf (A805/B833). The Bible is full of insights that address all three of Kant's questions. An important question that Kant does not raise is, What is real?
41. For a fine analysis of Luther's understanding of reason, see G. A. Gerrish, "Luther, Martin," in The Encyclopedia of Philosophy, ed. Paul Edwards (The Macmillan Co. and The Free Press, 1967), 5.109–113.
42. Any appeal to truth per se is uncomfortable for a postmodern mindset. Philosopher Richard Rorty captured that mindset when he argued that "truth is what your contemporaries let you get away with." However, in my experience subjectivism gives way to objective truth claims whenever a person gets the wrong change in a store. Then there is an objective truth that can be known and vociferously

argued for until the right change is given. For the Rorty quote, see Goodreads.com, https://www.goodreads.com/quotes/284543-truth-is-what-your-contemporaries-let-you-get-away-with. A simpler distinction I like is that between magisterial reason and instrumental reason. Magisterial reason makes the ego the adjudicator of all truth. Instrumental reason is reasoning in the service of the quest for truth.

43. Socrates, *Apology,* in *Great Dialogues of Plato*, eds. Eric H. Warmington and Philip G. Rouse (Mentor Books, 1956), 443: "Life without enquiry is not worth living for a man."
44. Rosaria Champagne Butterfield, "My Train Wreck Conversion," *Christianity Today*, February 7, 2013, http://www.christianitytoday.com/ct/2013/january-february/my-train-wreck-conversion.html?start=1.
45. Rosaria Champagne Butterfield, "You are What—and How—You Read," The Gospel Coalition, February 13, 2014, https://www.thegospelcoalition.org/article/you-are-whatand-howyou-read/.
46. Butterfield, "You are What—and How—You Read."
47. Quoted in Lindsey Carlson, "Rosaria Butterfield: Christian Hospitality is Radically Different from 'Southern Hospitality,'" *Christianity Today*, April 24, 2018, https://www.christianitytoday.com/ct/2018/april-web-only/rosaria-butterfield-gospel-comes-house-key.html.

48. When I review what I have written above, I feel like a travel writer. I am trying to describe a place that my reader may never have seen. That's why later in this book I give some tools for engaging with the Bible for yourself and how to visit Ely Cathedral in person.
49. A mental or written file of puzzles generated by reading Scripture and the experience of life that are awaiting further light (AFL).
50. Caitlin Casey is a scientist at the University of Texas. See Chris Baraniuk, "It took centuries, but we now know the size of the Universe," *BBC News*, June 13, 2016, http://www.bbc.com/earth/story/20160610-it-took-centuries-but-we-now-know-the-size-of-the-universe.
51. The text may be found in a modern English version at https://www.biblegateway.com/quicksearch/?quicksearch=John&qs_version=NIV.
52. This was the experience of philosopher Dallas Willard as an undergraduate. See Gary W. Moon, *Becoming Dallas Willard: The Formation of a Philosopher, Teacher and Christ Follower* (IVP, 2018), 63–64. Amazingly this experience took place in a laundromat as Willard began to read the Gospel of John to pass the time.
53. Peter Blowes, "The Swedish Method," The Briefing, January 1, 2009, http://matthiasmedia.com/briefing/2009/01/the-swedish-method/. Blowes

recommends reading a passage of 10–15 verses each time.

54. Blowes, "The Swedish Method." Blowes takes the method further with more symbols for those with some acquaintance with the Bible. He suggests "a set of circling arrows (to show the interrelation of ideas in the passage)." A heart symbol captures the central idea in the passage. A circle with an arrow coming out of the circle indicates the "innate central application."
55. A good resource for digging deeper is *NIV Zondervan Study Bible,* ed. D.A. Carson (Zondervan, 2015).
56. John Piper, *Glory*, 21.

Printed in the United States
by Baker & Taylor Publisher Services